Ripples

a collection of poetry

by

Colin Ward

Published by *In As Many Words*

www.inasmanywords.com

ISBN 978-1-9998089-2-1
Paperback

Cover & book design by Colin Ward

First printed February 2018

For you.

"Whether 'tis nobler in the mind to suffer
The slings and arrows of outrageous fortune,
Or to take arms against a sea of troubles
And by opposing end them."

William Shakespeare, Hamlet

Contents

Introduction

I think we all have times when we consider our place in the world and muse over the mark our lives might leave when we are gone. What have we achieved? Whose lives have we touched? Have we influenced or inspired those who have known us?

How will we be remembered?

Ripples is a collection of poems brought together as an exploration of these questions. I've deliberately given no context or explanation for any of the poems. Most of them have been written over the past few years, but it is only in this publication that I consider my part in their journey to be finished. I leave the rest up to you.

The poems are grouped into four loose sections, more as a suggestion of shared topics than a collective meaning. Parts One and Two are about stirring emotions and exploring the senses. Parts Three and Four share similar themes of politics, justice, seeking truth, and philosophy. These are merely a general guide, and not even strong enough to warrant thematic titles.

Whether the poetry moves you to smile, gasp, wonder or cry, I hope this collection creates a few tiny ripples in your thoughts.

Part 1

Fear

You
are the one
who locked me
in a darkened room

with no walls or doors;
held me high in the sky
shook away the floor;
rattled my teeth
and tightened my jaw;
trapped sandpaper whispers
beneath your gravelly roar;
grappled heart-thumping chest
with a burning claw;
squeezed at my throat
crushing the draw
of one last frozen breath
I could gasp at before,
through blood stained vision,
my eyes tight-shut saw
the end of my time

desperately pleading
to escape
life needing
you.

Smiles and Eyes

Smiles sit still under the eyes
which look with hope to find allies
forced-separated
into socially constipated
tables of
Smiles still sat under the eyes
no matter how hard anyone tries
to give ice-cold cues
tonne-weight clues
leaving
Smiles that still defy the eyes
as dignity finds true demise
empty promises shared
everyone socially scared
to say

I don't know you.
I don't want to know you.
I don't want to pretend to know you.

Hide Away

Shifting chameleon-like through colours,
escape being seen in light,
or noticed in shadows,
scurry away without a stir.

Existing regretfully alone,
bearing neither strength
nor nurtured will
to change or speak of.

Hard-faced against truth,
denying dilemmas,
lying to reflections,
simply surviving.

Self-destruct beyond repair,
not from less caring,
but more compassion,
for other lives.

Will belief ever be spirited
by enough freedom,
for enough hope,
to be more than just words?

A Muse
A Haiku

Youth must remember:
finding a muse meant giving
moments of laughter.

Sincerity
A Haiku

Breathe the delightful
fresh air of sincerity
gifted from true hearts.

Joy

Smile,
laugh,
joyful
memories
breathe life shimmering
wistfully glimmering freedom.

Sorry Solitude

Did you know
I always made you suffer
a sorry solitude?

I made you
walk alone in darkness,
locked in a mental fortress
of sorry solitude.

I gripped you
by both arms so harshly,
squeezed out the world so tightly,
dragged back your heart so roughly,
to sorry solitude.

I forced you
to thrash your wits as rapture,
hold no unworthy capture,
or forsake such self-torture,
let love have free feature,
not sorry solitude.

Did you know
it was me
here inside,
holding on
to a sad
silenced soul:
your sorry solitude?

Alone

Always a relentless nothing,
Life by the silent crown,
Oracles betray promised duty,
Nerve-shattered soul has learnt:
Expect no-one to gift salvation.

Loneliness

Do not speak to me out of pity
to fill a void today
when yesterday unprompted
would have meant more anyway.
Fear not the feeling
of *being* alone
but dread knowing
of *still* being
alone tomorrow.

Disposable

Words of fantasist liars
deemed credible and true;
no shred of evidence;
finger pointed at you.

Pilloried by ignorance;
torn apart by hacks;
blow by blow dismembered;
by visceral attack.

Left like waste all broken;
defeated to the core;
too much truth unspoken;
raped by moral whores.

Four Walls

A window with no view
four walls of stone, cave-like
strangling freedom dry,
noise of silence cries,
metal door of the mind slams.

Reflections

You
see
nothing
in darkened
reflections that hate
looking into tired, ageing eyes:
anywhere else is easier
except when it feels
deep enough
inside
the
soul.

Two Little Ducks

Ice cold silence swallowed the air
shadows leaked down
splintered and worn stairs
distressed by years of abuse
cracked ribs of balustrades struggle
to pull themselves to the top
where uneven feet turn sharp
dancing tired
creaking boards
loosened like bones of old
fear-fraught steps
leading to the bathroom
door hanging wearily
finger-tip hinges pinched the hang
slithered open just enough
dirty air thickened
by dusty shafts of light
sticking in the nose with damp
stinking heavy
from solid full roll-top
sitting sloth-like central
of the putrid pond
made satin by the congealed arm
held carefully by two little ducks
whose smiling eyes
welcomed the first wanderer
to discover the end.

Part 2

Perfect Body

Soft silken hair whispers in the wind;
dark crimson red waves, reflecting its glow,
complexion made from purest porcelain;
cream-smooth, duck egg shell
delicate to the touch, soft of aroma,
it curves the hour of art from top to toe.
breasts lie flat as nature made;
belly shaped for nourished life
but without lines of promise to another;
and yet the craft of dignity betrays no less attention
than this beauty would surely have commanded.
A face paused in a moment
with stunning blue eyes who lend their shade
to soft-curved lips, dry but not yet cracked.
A soft burgundy necklace
darkens as the sun goes down;
the moon turns the silk hair black
giving the eyes such depth
that I dig another level deeper
into nature's shell
to return this perfect body.

Trees Know Best

Trees know best
announcing Spring
blossom bloom for songbird sing
bodies growing thick
with soft fresh fingers to play tricks
by dealing light by slight of hand
eyes much lower strew the land
some fresh picking the season of fruit
days grow wider to occasion
the brute burn of rays

Yes, trees know best
to provide shade pockets
where couples may socket
lust in borrowed glow
fresh cut smells of kiss and tell
and hearts blossom wants to show
but trees know best.

And rustle to tell
of autumn on the crest
change in the breeze
a drizzle drops with ease
leaves leap from head to toe
gathered piles of promise
as their lives run dry
children small and big
perform dances of kick-dig
crunching the song of the land

until leaves drink deep
and finally life-leap
one last time
into slippery slime
lethal enough to make great engines fail
and collide
like a deadly tide
crest-fallen just after its peak
as it breaks.

And how the trees know best
to warn in naked show
beneath brave balanced snow
that holds on for dear life
to be noticed as beauty
worthy of life
before falling with more glory than the leaves
into the slurry below
punished by feet
of sludge-trudgers
whose lives are commanded
by her seasons demands

that the trees know best.

Door to the Promise Land

Across the darkened cool slate stands
the door of promise to some other land;
another place filled with desires
of mind and body, heart-warming fire.
Upon approach a soft, rolling hum
plays the mind like a brush-stroked drum
its steely face reflects the pain
driving anticipation insane
and as the hand takes determined hold
ready poised to reveal its gold
the gentlest tug does break the seal
and gasps to share a rich reveal.
First nothing shared but shadowed mystery
like a book that hopes to harbour history
the gentle swing bathes forth a light
glaring back eyes of the secret night
until full mission the view abides
what appetites have lay inside
as cool shivers ripple their escape
mist dispersed and world richly draped
shelf upon shelf of tongue-tingling treasures
no space unpacked; no inch half-measures
soul enriched by the joys within:
the good, the bad, and the worldly sins.

Belated

I know. It's late.
I'm sorry.
But the postman never collected
the envelope rejected
the stamp I couldn't buy
from the shop
that only sells books of twelve,
because it was closed
just as I arrived
at the card shop
which were busy
opening up
as I watched them
from behind my coffee and Danish
this morning.

Still: it's the thought that counts.

Magic

Quick
slip
vanish
fascinate
senses fluctuate
answers dissipate into smoke.

Linguistic Blunders

Devastating linguistic blunders
happen when falling under
wheels of meaning
which roll towards
futile reinvention
that drives no desires.

Expression

Expression is the joy of mind
growing with each cold retort
never shall it suffer a fate so unkind
until, brutally, its breath be cut sh…

The Dressmaker

Who else could conjure cotton frocks
from cotton socks
and overused jocks;
combining shirts of every girth
with suits from birth
coloured by earth;
held together by finger fumbler straps
worn out flaps
and unsightly gaps;
yet create such beauty for a one-day survive
and together-stitch two lives
for lucky-lover husbands and wives.

Delivery

It's nearly time,
they say.
It'll be just around the corner,
I know it's on the way,
sense the anticipation,
crippled but to say

I am expecting,
you see.
It'll be prompt on its arrival,
a promise made to me,
the word that I can stand by,
revered integrity.

And I'm certain,
I know,
there is no miscommunication,
or chance it will not show.
I have the word of honour
and nowhere else to go.

But I'm still waiting,
and fear,
that I have shared my faith too freely.
How long will I be here?
Developing disgruntled,
red mist now clouds the clear,

and it passes,
it's gone.
The guarantee is broken.
The clock has passed the one.
My anger outstrips my patience
now I know it's just a con.

All this time
waiting.
Hours wasted
waiting.
Nothing to show for
waiting.
But a little card
waiting
on the floor
waiting
for my return from
waiting
until nature called me from
waiting
a moment too long.

And now
the card says it will be
waiting
for me to collect after
waiting
until tomorrow.

Part 3

Too Little Too Late

Too little; too late
for him.
Too little to be lost.
Too lost to be saved.
Too innocent
to carry the guilt
he was given.
Too much, undeserved.
Too many words,
insincere;
Too few images
shared too much
to change opinion.
To weakly
justify;
to cowardly
dismiss;
to turn
two-faced.
Too little; too late
for pity.
Too little; too late
for him.

One Vile Lie

They are your child,
grandchild;
nephew or niece;
and one vile lie
shattered life to pieces.
A future now stolen,
hopes sent to scrap;
their innocence murdered
barely out of your lap

Squeeze tighter your hold,
their soul slips away,
quickly growing old,
holding hate at bay.
Words of razor wire,
burning your ears;
but no smoke and no fire
is put out by your tears.

They were your child,
grandchild;
nephew or niece;
and one vile lie
killed their Rest In Peace.

For False Truth

No crime has been committed
making this fate deserved
to bring upon this judgement
where justice was reserved.

Tallest tales are taken
society will shout
masking malice mistaken
a double-dose of doubt.

None will have borne witness
nor evidence afforded
to uncloud the oldest memory
for false truth to be applauded.

HypocriTory

Do you stand up for all
as you sit there judgemental
wanna protect your home
but move continental
where the rains don't fall
and drown so detrimental
that land you bemoan
but you're too sentimental
to turn your back
on misleading govern-mentals
who hide their dirty hands
behind claims it's accidental
that the maths don't match
some funding fundamentals
of truth?

Does your face still fit
even when it's double-sided
and smiles at your friends
as their back's being derided
sure of your assurance
but you know it's undecided
as you offer your trust
when your Loyalty's all lopsided
sordid secrets denied
because your promise is provided
on the back of the names
of the monumentally misguided
land you have no right
to have so dishonestly presided
with lies?

They Were Told

They were told they'd troop with honour
to defend our nation's grace;
how fortitude would be enough
to save the human race.

They were trained to fight with courage
being free would fuel their fire,
justify the loss of souls
with peace upon the pyre.

They were led to death with orders,
belief in righteous cries
to qualify the stolen truths
which bleed through tearful eyes.

Minds Made to Doubt

Tall tales drifting out
loosened thoughts running too fast
nowhere to escape.

Mysteries shout
painful truths that borrow pasts
hidden under capes.

Lies cause moral drought
leaving scars to ever last
in minds made to doubt.

Always Money for War

In these times of austerity
we should all give thanks:
the economy is growing,
strengthening the banks.
They may have taken all our money,
as the rich have robbed the poor,
but we should be grateful,
there's always money for war.

Our health service is a sinking ship,
doctors vote for first-time strikes,
Ministers still deal the cards
and now nurses face a funding hike;
paramedics race against the clock,
patients face the closing door
on mental, social or old age care:
yet there is always money for war.

Our children's minds are all but spent,
each name given is just penny-drawn
to leave the moving targets bare
just as good teachers warned
that time stripped thinner than snake-sheath spent
but all we hear is "Schools: do more"
and the young now fill un-working boots
Still: there is always money for war.

Why don't we ask how it has come to be,
we are left with unelected cheats
when one man's monthly heating bill
is spent each morning as an MP eats?
All our heroes, Lest We Forget,
whose sovereign duties we claim to adore,
can be left in squalor with no regret,
but there is always money for war.

They Shed no Tears for You

They shed no tears for you
hungry child.

You rub your weary stomach
and wonder when it's safe
to hunt for food again
in this strange unknown place.
Do it quietly
as nations stand
independently, but dependently,
in silence
in respect
of those long gone;
in remembrance
they salute pain and pride
and honour
of a service done,
a sacrifice given
in the voice of wars,
and the name of peace.
So many wars, despite
hiding behind modern excuses
that you must swallow
as all you will eat today:
'Lest we forget'
why our heroes died.

They shed no tears for you,
hungry child.

You are not known;
not big enough for history;
not hero enough to die
for your country
or for your public,
who need their voyeur's meal;
not molested by famed hands
or raped by God's speaker;
not pretty enough
to be in photos;
or different enough to be a quota;
privileged enough
to be on holiday
and be victim-chased,
more worthy-named
for not dying at home.

They shed no tears for you,
hungry child.

Malice Through the Looking Glass

She starts with a grin
to herself, she thinks
posing whore-like
wet hair dripping the first lie
spiderweb: it holds her youthful breast
that shall never tempt
nor suckle the innocence they should.
Poison pout of the slut
backhanded by her own hand
just hard enough to tell-tale
while the other hand creeps
miming the instrument
playing the evil tune
rehearsing the callous creation
she stares deep into voids
that know no bounds
to hold back hate,
blackest, blood-boiling hate
that her stone heart will never sense;
as blow by petulant blow
she torments truth,
tortures integrity
and in one foul cry of malice
propped up by the convenient ease
of righteous indignation,
stalwart ignorance of fact
she smashes through the looking glass
which crashes with other's blood

and falls to her feet
crouching cat-like with all nine lives
gingerly purr-picking
the most jagged-tooth edge
as she steps through the frame
to fuck his wife;
to murder his children;
to cut the throat of hope;
watch its life drain away,
mixing with crocodile tears
she stabs eyes that see;
slices ears that hear;
gouges minds that doubt
and question
her chameleon-calls;
ill-gotten gains
from her self-storied pains;
purging the need to feed
the sorrowful, sickening, suffering
stench so foul;
she shits on her own hands,
smothers Justice and pisses on her feet.
Widow-maker wench,
deceitful to the core,
putrid self-pity
enough to venom her victims,
then slither away unseen
back under Nature's rock
of depravity.

Part 4

Give us Pause

That we may come
and we may go
ghostlike through the ebb and flow
of days and weeks,
months and years,
through silenced speech and dried out tears.

That we must seek
and we must find
questions fit to open minds
to wake the world
and open eyes
so withered words become the cries.

That we can live
and we can die
running from the fear of why
our withered dreams
and stolen joys
could never grow our men from boys:

who give us pause
to understand.

Ripples

Life might be a single voyage
across an ocean filled with waves
that shake in journeys, ignoring buoys
and end upon a land that saves.

My soul can stay afloat so long
to keep but one breath ahead
sinking may seem to be so wrong
but being alive is merely a paddle from dead.

If all we know is in the sails
that stretch and challenge in a bow
and when our dreams do nothing but fail
must we accept our lot or just let go?

We can wish, and we can hope
to be more than a drop in the sea
but can we bear, or even cope
if there's nothing else that we can be?

A single drop pushes ripples wide
with no other place that they can go
than to follow along a moonlit tide
and finish on the grounds we know.

To move just one single grain of sand
might pave the way for futures untold
and we may not yet understand
how youthful ripples grow comfortably old.

But can we find an inner release,
if we're not an ocean, a sea, or lake,
or even a drop that drips in any of these
by some cruel and fateful mistake?

I don't mind,
because

I'd rather be a thousand ripples,
or even just the one,
than a single drop in a dreary abyss
drowned; forever gone.

Rules

A Haiku?

Sometimes life has rules
that must be challenged enough
to be reconsidered.

Superstition

In life I must reflect
on each chance I get to thrive
through all the chances I neglect,
and somehow still survive.

I stare black cats right in the eyes,
declare they dare to cross my luck,
but I refuse to muse upon demise
or give a frizzy feline fur...

'cause things go wrong; visions break,
and hope begins to shatter,
but I don't care for a ladder mistake
like life itself won't matter.

Uncertainty

I want

to make time stand still
for a moment longer than it should
to be hard to hear
when screaming something bad or good
to leave people blind
like there's nothing they'd want to see
to have questions asked
about what life is supposed to be.

I want
the world
to embrace
uncertainty.

Hours, Days & Weeks

Where do all the hours
days
and weeks
go?
What happened to life's to-and-fro?
Ups and downs,
fooling around,
the joyous adventure
of a symphony of sounds,
comfort in silence
when none was around,
and now this.

My partner in crime
was released
as I fought for justice
shouted for
unheard voices,
raged against that which
offends
our every value
we owe to
Nature.

Whilst back in the shadows,
untold to my world,
a voice has since faded,
final song has been sung.
These are the days, weeks, months,
and longer still:
unspoken stubborn sorrow
wrapped the darkness
around the light
and waved
our belated goodbye.

Lurking Words

Heavy bootsteps tell of ominous approach
hidden behind the old door.
Paint peeling,
handle squealing,
light barely cast from

the window open, just slightly enough
to let spring morning breeze dance
with singing starling
who joyfully bring
a warmth felt

by lust-filled drink of life drawn,
beauty drained white as cream
turning grey,
gasped away,
morbidly felt

like the old story-teller's touch,
sat by fire warming more than skin.
Smiles wise,
deep eyes,
live richly until

tongues trip over ancient tomes,
neither gained nor gifted,
faith filled,
duty spilled,
sense of self;
redacted.
silent.

Words left to lurk in shadows
meander meaningless through mindless meadows
towards creation
in relation
to nothing.

Drive

Cocooned by this journey I must make
trapped by a twist of fate
deserved for all it says about
my one, single act of betrayal and broken trust,
which now serves too many paths
that can never meet.
I walk away
without turning my back:
nothing more than a wish
that I might return to that which I forgot
in one careless, selfish act of misplaced kindness.
As integrity is laid bare for all to see in all its shame,
I follow this hallowed lane
that leads me towards the fear I have spent my life trying
to escape.
Reputation cannot rescue respect
if dignity is demised by a dalliance with desire.
One moment my eyes closed to my soul
and flooded my heart with the
poisonous partners of pity and prurience.
History counts for nothing if it betrays a future,
even with the beauty and miracle of life.
Yet, with all the pain and tears this act will cause,
just to deliver a moment of comfort,
I cannot, I must not
deny the duty towards deceit
for that which I did not plan;
but whose plan now unwinds my world

like wires barbed with the rusty knowledge
that in order to commit one single act of good;
to do what I know to be right
I must serve up sufferance,
risk failure for those who afforded faith
harm those whose love plays the beats of my heart
and drive
knowing
I can never return
the same man I was before
but
hope that I might become
more than the man I always refused to be.

Dreams

I lie, still awake,
wondering at a life spent
stood still in my dreams.

Stand Alone

If faith must make you apologise
can belief not stand alone?
Do hearts not see with their own eyes?
If faith must make you apologise
and forgive for all forced fearful cries,
how is it that man's heart has grown?
If faith must make you apologise,
can belief not stand alone?

Do Not Wait Until Tomorrow

Do not wait until tomorrow
to celebrate joy
or set aside sorrow;
to deliver on a promise
or return a belated borrow;
to chase the distant dream
or be guide to those who follow

your ambition to fulfil
a heart that hurts so hollow,
for trusting what must hold true:

do not wait until tomorrow
because tomorrow never waits for you.

Acknowledgements

Special thanks to *Patricia M Osborne*, a fellow author, for editing the collection, and the many hours spent sharing ideas about all things to do with writing.

Also, to the unsung heroes of my writing career: the teachers in some of my most formative years, especially throughout my A-Levels. It was their passion for the English language that sowed the long-overdue seeds which finally brought me to publish this first collection. I've written stories, plays, musicals, songs, and a novel. Now I've taken a dive into the *"sea of troubles"* – poetry.

Other Works by the Author

"To Die For"

An action-packed crime thriller set in Birmingham, where a killer's thirst for blood forces DI Mike Stone to investigate the darkness of humanity itself.

CHASING ECHOES OF CRIES HE'D SPENT A LIFETIME TRYING TO SILENCE.

A KILLER TELLING A SINISTER STORY
DI Mike Stone investigates an unusual murder. It quickly becomes clear that the killer has only revealed the first brutal chapter.

A DETECTIVE FIGHTING A DARK DAEMON
The case takes on a disturbing speed as Stone finds his professional and personal worlds colliding, exposing a painful past, and threatening his future.

A CONNECTION WITH A TERRIFYING TRUTH
Who is this case really about? How far must Stone go to uncover the truth? And at what cost?

Find out more about the writer on his website

www.inasmanywords.com

and on social media as

@inasmanywords
&
@colinwardwriter